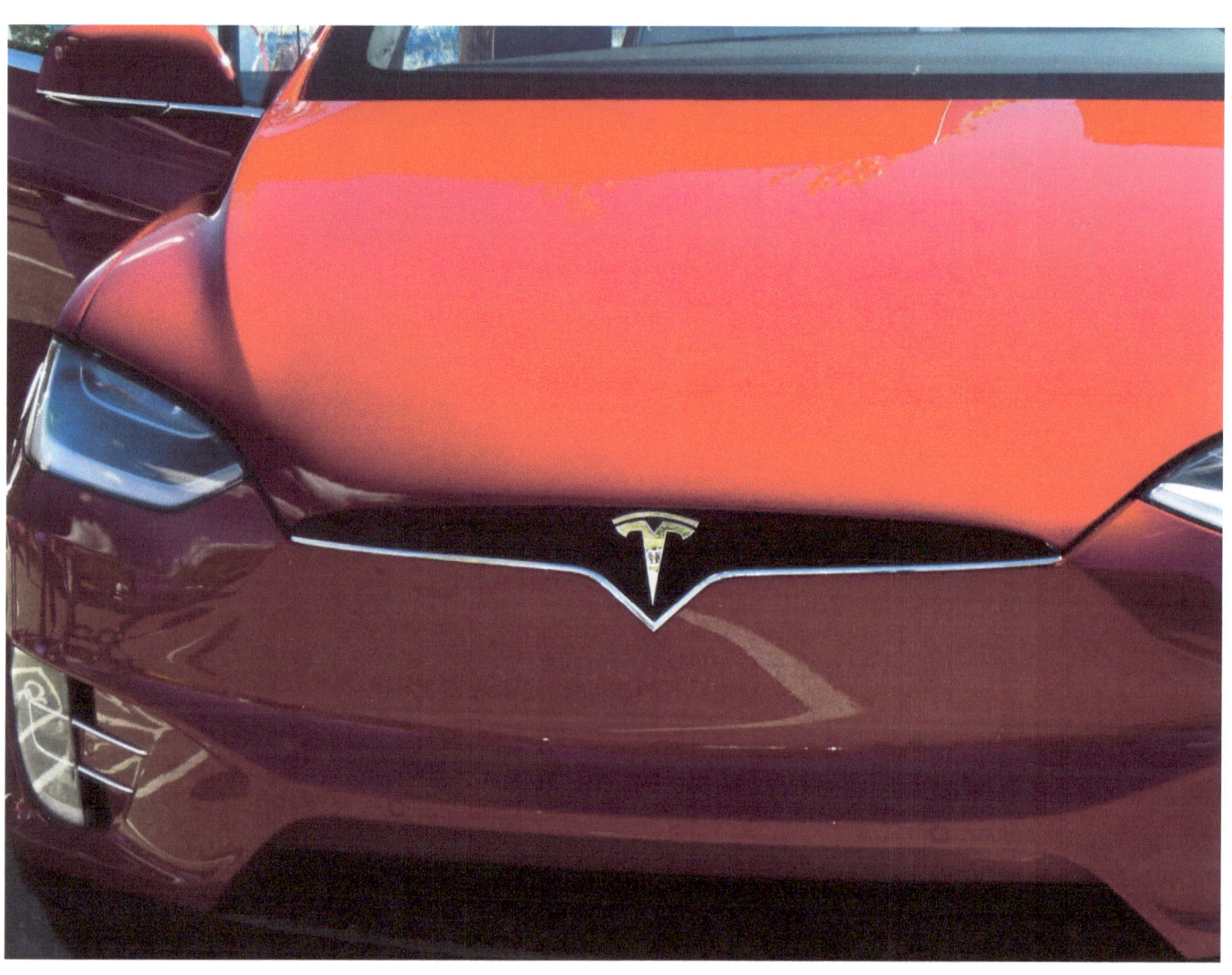

Alright its not a car but its still really cool.

More on kindle books by this auther

www.ingramcontent.com/pod-product-compliance
Lightning Source LLC
Chambersburg PA
CBHW051048180526
45172CB00002B/553